REVELATION

The Mercy Seat of God

WILLIAM T. SMITH

NEWMAN SPRINGS PUBLISHING
320 Broad Street
Red Bank, NJ 07701

First originally published by Newman Springs Publishing 2021

This book came from my heart and on what I have read and heard—the Holy Bible KJV, the things I read in newspapers and heard on television, messages I heard from the pulpit, *Young's Bible Dictionary*, *The Concise A to Z Guide to Finding It in the Bible*, *Illustrated Dictionary and Concordance of the Bible*, Lifeway's *Adult Learner Guide*, and Lifeway's *Adult Explore the Bible*.

ISBN 978-1-63692-700-8 (Paperback)
ISBN 978-1-63692-701-5 (Digital)

Printed in the United States of America

To my God, Jesus, my Savior; also to my family and friends; and my church family who encouraged me to keep going.

A special thanks to the ministers who preach God's Word.

A special thanks to my brother Jim Smith, whose book *Nuggets of Gold* (ISBN 978-0-692-06545-7), and my nephew Herbie Smith, whose book *Keepers of the Dawn* (e-book only) keep inspiring me to write.

My thanks and prayers be with you all. Amen.

William T. Smith

A NOTE FROM THE AUTHOR

I wish to thank my Lord and Savior for this book.

I wish to honor my Lord Jesus for He is the one sitting on the Mercy Seat of God.

My hope and prayer is this: if you do not know Jesus as your Savior, you will want to after reading this book.

My hope is that you will also write about Jesus and your experience in accepting Him, as well as having faith in Jesus.

William T. Smith

PREFACE

I would like to speak to the ministers and laypersons: If you speak and preach Jesus Christ as virgin birth; having a righteous life; going through a terrible, agonizing death; having a glorious resurrection; and a triumphant return for forty days, which gave us a marvelous Holy Spirit, then I do applaud you. If not, don't you think it is about time you did?

To the unbeliever, I want you to know that Jesus Christ loves you. My prayer is this: Heavenly Father, let the person that reads this realize that they do need a savior. This savior is Jesus Christ, the one who died on the cross for all the sins we committed. If you would like to receive Jesus Christ as your personal Savior, this is how it is done: "Believe on the Lord Jesus Christ and you shall be saved, and your house as well" (Acts 16:31).

You first have to believe in your heart that Jesus is God and would like Him to be Lord of your life. Ask Jesus to forgive you for the sins you have committed against Him. In asking and believing, Lord Jesus will become your master, king, and Father God. This is called repenting and becoming a child of God, where before, Lucifer—better known as Satan or the devil—was your prince, master, and god.

MERCY SEAT

There is a seat on the right side of the Heavenly Father. Only one person can sit thereon and no other.

The seat is called Mercy Seat of God where Jesus sits. For Jesus knew what each of us did and what we think. Because of these wrong things that we do in this life, we deserve to be in hell—separated from God and being in strife. But Jesus said He will go to earth as an advocate for us that whosoever believes in Jesus will no longer be dead.

"I will have mercy on that person before my Heavenly Father and will make them heirs to my throne as my brother."

Therefore, all who accepts Jesus as their Savior will be in glory. All you need to do is ask for forgiveness and be truly sorry.

The dead that is in Christ will be fully resurrected. When you were separated from Jesus, you are dead.

Jesus said we are dead, without hope, following the world. When we say YES to Jesus, we are raised into a new life.

William T. Smith

BORN AGAIN

Have you ever wondered what the phrase "born again" means? The Bible records that Jesus used the Phrase in a conversation with a man named Nicodemus. Nicodemus approached Jesus at night. He was curious about Jesus and the kingdom of God.

Jesus told him: "Unless someone is born again, he cannot see the kingdom of God" (John 3:3).

Nicodemus responded, "But how can anyone be born when he is old?" (John 3:4).

Nicodemus was a highly moral man who obeyed God's law. He was a respected leader of the Jewish community. No doubt he was a fine man. Yet something was lacking. Like Nicodemus, many people today confuse religion with new birth in Christ. Phrases like "I believe there is a God" often are confused with a real new-birth experience.

New birth begins with the Holy Spirit convicting a person that the person is a sinner. Because of sin, we are spiritually dead. For this reason, spiritual birth, as Jesus described it, is necessary. God loves us and gives us spiritual birth when we ask Him for it.

The Bible says all persons are sinners (Romans 3:23). Jesus died on a cross and was raised from the dead to save sinners. To be born again means that a person admits to God that he or she is a sinner, repents of sin, believes in or trust Christ, and confesses faith in Christ as Savior and Lord. Jesus told Nicodemus that everyone that who believes in (places faith in) Christ would not perish (John 3:16).

Jesus is the only One who can save us (John 14:6).

Jesus Christ was with God the Father before the world was created. He became human and lived among humanity as Jesus of Nazareth. He came to show us what God the Father is like. He lived a sinless life, showing us how to live; and He died upon across to pay for our sins. God raised Him from the dead.

Jesus is the source of eternal life. Jesus wants to be the doorway to new life for you. In the Bible He was called the "Lamb of God" (John 1:29). In the Old Testament, sacrifices were made for sins of the people. Jesus became the sacrificial lamb offered for your sin.

Jesus said, "I am the way, the truth, and the life. No one comes to the Father except through Me" (John 14:6). He is waiting for you now.

Admit to God that you are a sinner, Repent, turning away from your sin.

By faith receive Jesus Christ as God's Son and accept Jesus' gift of forgiveness from sin. He took the penalty for your sin by dying on the cross.

Confess your faith in Jesus Christ as Savior and Lord.

To believe in Jesus is to be born again. Confess your sins and ask Jesus right now to save you. "Whoever calls on the name of the Lord will be saved" (Acts 2:21).

You may say a prayer similar to this as you call on God to save you:

"Dear God, I know that You love me. I confess my sin and need of salvation. I turn away from my sin and place my faith in Jesus as my Savior and Lord. In Jesus' name I pray, Amen".

After you have received Jesus Christ into your life, tell a pastor or another Christian you have received Jesus Christ into your life, share your decision with another person, and following Christ's example, ask for baptism by immersion in your local church as a public expression of your faith (Romans 6:4; Colossians 2:6).

Explore the Bible
LifeWay

CHAPTER 1

As I was sitting on the porch, listening and watching the birds sing and fly, my thoughts went to, *How do these birds fly, and what makes them sing so beautifully?* This question may have been a simple one, but the answer is very complex. The only and best way I can answer a question of this nature is to look into the book called the Holy Bible. This is the answer I found.

In the beginning there is a God. This God created everything you see and what you cannot see. But before God created the birds and the way they sing and fly, God had to do something else that was much bigger. The first thing He did was to create a place called heaven and a place called earth. Now in this heaven, which is God's heavenly home, He created three angels to care for it, which He called archangels. God named these three angels Gabriel, Michael, and Lucifer.

Gabriel—he is a messenger angel who delivers messages to the other angels as well as those that was put on the earth. Now in order for Gabriel to do all of this, he had to have help. So God created more angels to help him in this task. As you know, this is a very big and important job. Gabriel did this with the help of the angels he was in charge of.

Another one of these angels is Michael. Michael was in charge of keeping the peace. Just like man, God gave angels the right to choose—to obey or not. So this meant that if the angel Gabriel sent out did not want to deliver that message then Michael would come in and correct the situation. Now this was a big order for Michael to do alone. So God created another band of angels to help Michael keep the peace. As we look around at our leaders, we all know keeping the peace is a very important to any leader. God is no different;

God also wants peace to exist with all of his creation. Michael did this with the help of the angels he was in charge of.

Another one of these angels is Lucifer. Lucifer had the most important job there is in heaven. This job was to protect what is known as the Mercy Seat of God. This brings up the question, What is the Mercy Seat of God? This is a very good question and one that we need to know. So I will try and explain this question; but in order to do so, I must put on hold the first question, How do birds fly, and what makes them sing so beautifully? I am very pleased and happy to explain this, for it will help me to answer the first question.

For this, we have to start at the beginning of creation—when God created the heaven and the earth. The very first thing God did after the creation was to put on His right side of his throne a seat, the Mercy Seat of God. This is a very special seat and made for only one person to sit on, the One Who Is Just and Righteous. This person had to be that—just and righteous—and no one else could sit there. This Mercy Seat was assigned to Lucifer the Archangel. God gathered His angels and let them know that the person had to be of earth but also of the heavenly realm.

Before I go any further: I looked in the dictionary for the definition of mercy seat. This is what I found. The *Webster's New Collegiate Dictionary* had this to say:

> mercy seat:
> 1) The gold plate resting on the ancient Jewish ark according to the account in Exodus.
> 2) The Throne of God.

Even though these were excellent definitions, I wasn't satisfied with this. So I looked in the *Young's Bible Dictionary*, and this is what it had to say:

> The mercy seat is the gold lid on the Ark of the Covenant of the testimony. The lid is called "the propitiary" (hakkapporet, AV "mercy seat").

Even though these are also very good definitions, they are not the version of what is in heaven. You may understand this better when we get closer to the end of this book. Now I would like to finish my story about Lucifer and the Mercy Seat.

Lucifer was put in charge to protect the Mercy Seat of God. So being the person to sit on it was coming from earth, Lucifer had to also protect earth as well. This is why it was the most important job in all heaven and earth. Lucifer needed a lot of help. So God created many angels to help in this protection. This meant that Lucifer had to be in heaven as well as on earth. This is why he had to have so many angels to help him. Not because of sin, for at this time, there was no sin. You can find this written in the book of Ezekiel 28:11–19.

Earth was very different from the way it is today. This earth was very beautiful, for there was no killing of animals for sin because there was no sin on the earth or in heaven. All creatures lived in harmony with each other. For there was also no killing of animals for food or clothing. God let them eat off the trees and plants; God also clothed them with humility. This made Lucifer's job much easier, for this earth was before the time as we know it today. On this earth, God did not need time or space because God was the time and space—also the light and heat for the earth.

Here is where the story starts to get very interesting: Lucifer was protecting the Mercy Seat so well that God rewarded him with special jewels and gifts. The gifts Lucifer received made him very beautiful, for the workmanship of thy tabrets and thy pipes was prepared in thee. And the jewels were his covering—the sardius, topaz, and the diamond; the beryl, the onyx, and jasper; the sapphire, the emerald, and the carbuncle; and gold. All of this made him not only beautiful but also very powerful, which led to envy, which led to desire and lust. Here was the cherub that covereth; and because iniquity was found in him, he wanted to sit in the seat, not just to protect it.

After Lucifer received his ninth jewel, God called his three archangels in for a conference. God asked his angels to search heaven and earth for the One Who Is Just and Righteous. This job was tough, for every angel and every creature on earth knew they were the one to sit on the Mercy Seat of God. So each of them went before the twenty-four elders who was in heaven around the Throne of God. But none of them was considered just or righteous. After searching high and low throughout heaven and earth, there was no one found to sit on the Mercy Seat. Lucifer started to think that he was the one. After all, wasn't he the most powerful and the most beautiful in all heaven and earth? And that was his first mistake, which led to sin.

Lucifer's mistake or sin was pride—that is, he thought himself to be better than anyone or anything else. So Lucifer went before the elders, and of course, they found him unworthy to sit on the Mercy Seat of God. Lucifer could not understand why. After all, wasn't he the most beautiful and the most powerful angel that was in all creation? Just because you are beautiful or powerful does not mean you are special enough to do whatever you wish or desire to do. When you do, that is pride, and the Word says that pride goes before a fall (Proverbs 16:18). That is what happened to Lucifer. And what came next was envy. Now if pride is against God's personality, what do you think envy is going to be? The dictionary has this to say:

> malice:
>> painful or resentful awareness of an advan-
>> tage enjoyed with a desire to possess the
>> same advantage

When envy comes into play, your mind starts to think about things that was never meant to be. This is what happened to Lucifer. He started to think that God and the twenty-four elders made a mistake and it was really him that should be sitting on the Mercy Seat of God. Envy mixed with pride makes a person or angel do things that he knows is wrong but just can't help but think it is right. When you put the two together…you guessed it. Pride made Lucifer think he was better than anyone or anything else. Envy made him think God and the elders made a mistake (we know that God never makes mistakes), but Lucifer was going to fix that mistake the only way he knew he could. That led to desire and lust. For you see, desire and lust are really about the same thing. You desire something so much you think you cannot live without it, and then it becomes lust. Desire and lust will put into action what envy only thinks about doing. That is why God does not like a person to become prideful or envious or lustful, for in doing so, it will lead to trouble and a big downfall.

Desire and lust put into action what should never be or supposed to happen in the first place. For Lucifer desired what—that if he could not sit on the Mercy Seat, then no one was going to. Lucifer knew the one had to be of earth as well as heaven, and Lucifer did not wish this to be so. Because of that thought, Lucifer went about to destroy the earth that was so precious to God, and that is what he proceeded to do. Lucifer had to convince the angels under him to rebel against God. As a result of this rebellion, Lucifer's name was changed to Satan, the Devil, the Evil One, the Dragon, or the Son of Perdition. For he did what he set out to do: to destroy the earth to the point that the earth became void and without form.

Now there was only one thing left to do before the Just and Righteous One could appear. God has to reestablish the earth in a way that Satan could not destroy it again. To protect the earth from being destroyed, God put His Spirit over the waters. After that, God put His Light in the earth. Without God's Spirit or His Light, nothing could live or know the right things to do. For now, sin had entered heaven, and God knew that sin would also reach earth. God thought of this before He even created the heaven and earth and had a way of escape for the human race. Being sin was in heaven at this time, Satan and his followers had to be ejected from heaven. There was a war at that time, and Satan lost and was thrown down to earth as the prince of the air.

CHAPTER 2

In the garden of Eden, God created a man called Adam and later his wife, Eve. They lived happily together, communing with God. But one day, Lucifer who is now Satan showed up and started to tempt Eve. He showed up as a serpent and enticed Eve to eat of the forbidden fruit. This sin as well as all sin is a disobedience against God. In doing so caused all people to be sinners.

Webster's New Collegiate Dictionary has this to say about sin:

1) a: an offense against religious or moral law
   b: an action that is or is felt to be highly reprehensible
2) a: transgression of the law of God.
   B: a vitiated state of human nature in which the self is estranged from God.

My definition of sin is this: doing something that causes you to be separated from the love of God, our Creator.

Therefore to him that knoweth to do good, and doeth it not, to him it is sin. (James 4:20)

For the invisible things of him from creation of the world are clearly seen, being understood by the things that are made, even his eternal power and Godhead; so that they are without excuse. (Romans 1:20)

If we say that we have not sinned, we make him a liar, and his word is not in us. (1 John 1:10)

Wherefore, as by one man entered into the world, and death by sin; and so death passed upon all men, for that all have sinned. (Romans 5:12)

A naughty person, a wicked man, walketh with a froward mouth. He winketh with his eyes, he speaketh with his feet, he teacheth with his fingers; Frowardness shall he be broken without remedy. (Proverbs 6:12–15)

And the tongue is a fire, a world of iniquity: so is the tongue among our members, that it defileth the whole body, and setteth on fire the course of nature; and it is set on fire of hell. For every kind of beasts; and of birds, and of serpents, and of things in the sea, is tamed, and hath been tamed of mankind: But the tongue can no man tame; it is unruly evil, full of deadly poison. (James 3:6–8)

Why do ye not understand my speech? Even because ye cannot hear my word. Ye are of your father the devil, and the lust of your father ye will do. He was a murderer from the beginning, and abode not in truth, because there is no truth in him. When he speaketh a lie, he speaketh of his own: for he is a liar, and the father of it. (John 8:43–44)

He that committeth sin is of the devil; for the devil sinneth from the beginning. (1 John 3:8)

But after thy hardness and impenitent heart treasurest up unto thyself wrath against the day of wrath and revelation of the righteous judgment of God; Who will render to every man according to his deeds. (Romans 2:5–6)

But if ye have respect to persons, ye commit sin, and are convinced of the law as transgressors. For whosoever shall keep the whole law, and yet offend in one point, he is guilty of all. (James 2:9–10)

As it is written, There is none righteous, no not one: There is none that understandeth, there is none that seeketh after God. For all have sinned, and come short of the glory of God. (Romans 3:10–11,23)

For when ye were the servants of sin, ye were free from righteousness. What fruit had ye then in those things whereof ye are now ashamed? For the end of those things is death. (Romans 6:20–21)

For if a man think himself to be something, when he is nothing, he deceiveth himself. For every man shall bear his own burden. Be not deceived; God is not mocked: for whatsoever a man soweth, that shall he also reap. For he that soweth to his flesh shall of the flesh reap corruption. (Galatians 6:3,5,7–8a)

Now the works of the flesh are manifest, which are these; Adultery, fornication, uncleanness, lasciviousness, idolatry, witchcraft, hatred, variance, emulations, wrath, strife, seditions, heresies, envyings, murders, drunkenness, revellings, and such like: of which I tell you before, as I have also told you in time past, that they which do such things, shall not inherit the Kingdom of God. (Galatians 5:19–21)

For this cause God gave them up unto vile affections: for even their women did change the natural use into that which is against nature: And likewise also the men, leaving the natural use of the woman, burned in their lust one toward another; men with men working that which is unseemly, and receiving in themselves that recompence of their error which was meet. And even as they did not like to retain God in their knowledge, God gave them over to a reprobate mind, to do those things which are not convenient; Being filled with all unrighteousness, fornication, wickedness, covetousness, maliciousness, full of envy, murder, debate, deceit, malignity; whispers, backbiters, haters of God, despiteful, proud, boasters, inventors of evil things, disobedient to parents, without understanding, covenant breakers, without natural affection, implacable, unmerciful: Who knowing the judgment of God, that they which commit such things are worthy of death, not only do the same, but have pleasure in them that do them. (Romans 1: 26–32)

But these speak evil of those which they know not: but what they know naturally, as brute beasts, in those things they corrupt themselves. Woe unto them! For they have gone in the way of Cain, and ran greedily after the error of Balaam for reward, and perished in the gainsaying of Core. (Jude 10–11)

But every man is tempted, when he is drawn away of his own lust, and enticed. Then when lust hast conceived, it bringeth forth sin: and sin, when it is finished, bringeth forth death. (James 1:14–15)

For we must all appear before the judgment seat of Christ; that every one may receive the things done in his body, according to that he hath done, whether it be good or bad. (2 Corinthians 5:10)

For let not man think that he shall receive any thing of the Lord. (James 1:7)

There is a way which seemeth right unto a man, but the end thereof are the ways of death. (Proverbs 14:12)

Nay, ye do wrong, and defraud, and that your brethren. Know ye not the unrighteous shall not inherit the kingdom of God? Be not deceived: neither fornicators, nor idolaters, nor adulterers, nor effeminate, nor abusers of themselves with mankind, nor thieves, nor covetous, nor drunkards, nor revilers, nor extortioners, shall inherit the kingdom of God. (1 Corinthians 6:8–10)

Woe unto the wicked! It shall be ill with him: for the reward of his hands shall be given him. (Isaiah 3:11)

O death, where is thy sting? O grave, where is thy victory? The sting of death is sin; and the strength of sin is the law. (1 Corinthians 15:55–56)

Now this I say, brethren, that flesh and blood cannot inherit the kingdom of God;

neither; does corruption inherit incorruption. (1 Corinthians 15:50)

But there were false prophets also among the people, even as there shall be false teachers among you, who privily shall bring in damnable heresies, even denying the Lord that bought them, and bring upon themselves swift destruction. And many shall follow their pernicious ways: by reason of whom the way of truth shall be evil spoken of. (2 Peter 2:1–2)

The Son of man shall send forth his angels, and they shall gather out of his kingdom all things that offend, and them which do iniquity: And shall cast them into a furnace of fire: there shall be wailing and gnashing of teeth. (Matthew 13:41–42)

What does all these scriptures mean? Here is a condensed version that might make more sense to you.

He that commits sin is of the devil; for the devil sinned from the beginning.

For we must all appear before the judgment seat of Christ; that every one may receive the things done in his body, according to that he has done; whether it was good or bad.

Who will render to every person according to their deeds.

As it is written, There is none that seek after God. For all have sinned, and come short of the glory of God.

> Wherefore, as by one man sin entered into
> the world, and death by sin, and so death passed
> upon all people, for that all have sinned.

You were altogether born in sin, and the Word teaches us that. And for that saying, they cast Jesus out because every person shall bear his own burdens.

The Bible says: "We all have sinned and come short of the glory of God," because of Adam and Eve's disobedience. We are sinners on this planet.

The Bible says: "We are strangers and foreigners to Christ the Messiah." That is because we are obedient to the god of the flesh.

The Bible says: "He that commit sin is of the Devil." So everything we say and do is from Lucifer, the evil one.

The Bible says: "No one is righteous; no not one." That is because we cannot receive righteous on our own. Our righteousness has to come from somewhere else; we can never be righteous.

The Bible says: "Sin and death has come unto all men." For all men are a product of temptation and sin.

The Bible says: "We are judged according to our deeds; whether what we have done is good or bad." Who can be good all the time? No one I know of, especially me, because we are all subject to the fruit of the flesh.

The Bible says: "We shall bear the sin of our own burdens." For there is a yoke around our neck, the yoke of sin; we are sinners. And being sinners, we have to pay for the sins we do; we cannot give them to anybody else.

The Bible says: "We are born in sin so we are sinners." Whereby comes this saying, "Once in sin, we are always in sin."

I, for one, am very glad God did NOT stop there. My God sent Jesus to earth. He took my punishment instead so that I would be covered by His mercy and grace and so that when I am judged, God will only see the righteousness of His Son, Jesus.

27

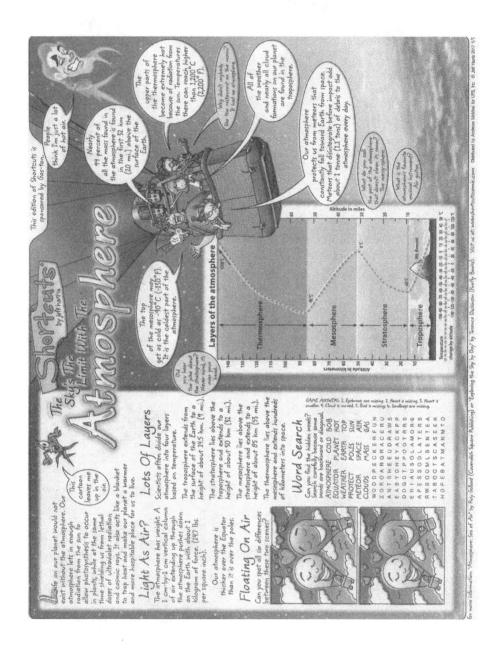

CHAPTER 3

God's Light is the life of earth, in that it gives the warmth to the soil, which is found in the center of the earth known as the core. This core is very hot and turns everything into liquid at a temperature of 2,200 degrees. This keeps the planet warm so things can grow. As a safeguard, God put three layers of rock to keep it from burning up. These layers of rock are known as asthenosphere, lithosphere, and fault blocks or better known as oceanic crust. God also put a protection on the outside of the earth in what we call space. Here, there are four layers known as thermosphere, mesosphere, stratosphere, and troposphere, with the thermosphere getting to the temperature of 2,200 degrees.

In this way, God is protecting the earth from everything that might come about. God did this so that the Just and Righteous One could be born on the earth, just as God said he would be. All of this was not done by accident; it had to happen just this way. Now Jesus, the Just and Righteous One, could be the redemption of the whole human race. Every creed and color found on earth can be forgiven of their sin.

Now that the earth was protected from the inside as well as from the outside, God was now ready to replenish the earth with animals and plants. In order to do this, God had to bring all the land into one place. This way, he could put trees and plants on it so that mankind and animals would be able to eat and breathe.

After this, God put the sun, moon, and the stars in the universe for days, seasons, and time as we know it today. Now that this was done, God started making the animals and fish and, last but not the least, mankind. Now the stage was set for the Just and Righteous of God (Jesus) to appear. But as righteous as Adam was, he still was not able to sit on the Mercy Seat of God. The reason Adam could not sit on the Mercy Seat is because Adam disobeyed God and he and his wife, Eve, ate of the forbidden fruit from the tree of good and evil that God told them not to eat from. This is still not the end of the story, for no one was able to sit on the Mercy Seat of God.

It took about six thousand years before someone could fulfill this task. This happened in a very special way. I will give you a little bit that led up to this glorious event. On the sixth day of creation, God told man to have dominion over the fish, the birds, the animals, and the plants; but what God wanted man to do was to multiply in the earth. After this, God rested, for it was on the seventh day, to which man should work six days and rest on the seventh. As God was resting and watching man, that is when God said it is time for the Just and Righteous One to be on the Mercy Seat. So God made Adam from His likeness, and God put this Adam in a garden so he could name all the animals that walked by him. Then God said: "It is not good that man is alone. I will make a help meet for him. I will do this by taking a rib from Adam and make a woman [whom Adam called Eve]." Adam and Eve worked and played in the garden. Until one day, Satan came into the garden portraying a serpent to deceive Adam and Eve.

Lucifer knew he could not destroy the garden or the man whom God put in charge of it. So Lucifer, or Satan as he is called, had to come up with a new plan. The plan that Lucifer thought of was to destroy man from the inside, being he couldn't from the outside. With this thought, Lucifer began his planning. God planted in the middle of the garden a tree called good or evil. "This tree," God told Adam, "do not to eat the fruit thereof for you will surely die. All the other trees in the garden you may eat of the fruit." God put this tree there as a reminder of what happened to the earth the first time. Knowing this, Lucifer entered into the mind of the serpent. As he was speaking through the serpent, Satan got Adam and Eve to eat of the forbidden fruit.

As a result, both Adam and Eve were kicked out of the garden because of Lucifer's action. The garden was removed from the earth, and a war started in heaven. The angels of Lucifer was fighting against the angels of Michael and Gabriel. When all was done, Lucifer and his angels were thrown out of heaven. Lucifer's name was changed to the Evil One, or the Devil, or Satan, or the Dragon, just to name a few.

All of this was done according to the plan of God, for Adam had to fall from mercy so that grace could appear. This someone had to be born from earth and be of Adam's descendant to be able to give grace unto the world. He also had to be of the heavenly realm in order to sit on the Mercy Seat of God. In the next six thousand years, there would be many people that would rise up in mercy but would fall from grace—none of them was the chosen one.

During all this time, the angels kept looking for the one to sit on the Mercy Seat of God. For six thousand years, it did not happen. But then two thousand years ago, someone did appear that was worthy. In order for this one to sit on the Mercy Seat of God, He had to open seven seals that only the chosen one could open. He came to earth as a baby. This baby was named Jesus (the Chosen One, Christ, Messiah, Son of God). As it is written in Isaiah 9:6–7, the Messiah, who is the anointed one, will come to save the world. Jesus of Nazareth is this anointed one, in that His life was perfect in all His ways and He was just in all the activities He did, from healing and all the preaching and teaching He did.

CHAPTER 4

In order for the Messiah to save the world, He had to take the punishment for all sin. Sin is the disobedience of God's Word that we humans do because of Adam and Eve disobeying God in the garden of Eden. Here are some verses that talk about that punishment Jesus took in our place—the punishment for the sins that we do against God, our Creator. We sin because we do not have a relationship with God, our Heavenly Father. So now we have those sins in our life from the time we were born.

> Surely he hath borne our griefs, and carried our sorrows: yet we did esteem him stricken, smitten of God, and afflicted. But he was wounded for our transgressions, he was bruised for our iniquities: the chastisement of our peace was upon him; and with his stripes we are healed, All we like sheep have gone astray: We have turned ever one to his own way; and the Lord hath laid on him the iniquity of us all. He was oppressed, and he was afflicted, yet he opened not his mouth: he is brought as a lamb to the slaughter, and as a sheep before the shearers is dumb, so he opened not his mouth. He was taken from prison and from judgment: and who shall declare his generation? For he was cut out of the living: for the transgression of my people was he stricken. And he made his grave with the wicked, and with the rich in his death; because he had done no violence, neither was any deceit in his mouth. (Isaiah 53:4–9)

And if ye call on the Father, who without respect of persons judgeth according to every man's work, pass the time of your sojourning here in fear: For as much as ye know that ye were not redeemed with corruptible things, as silver and gold, from your vain conversation received by tradition from your fathers; But with the precious blood of Christ, as of a lamb without blemish and without spot. (1 Peter 1:17–19)

For even hereunto were ye called: because Christ also suffered for us, leaving us an example, that ye should follow his steps: Who did no sin, neither was guile found in his mouth: Who, when he was reviled, reviled not again; when he suffered, he threatened not; but committed himself to him that judgeth righteously: Who his own self bare our sins in his own body on the tree, that we, being dead to sins, should live unto righteousness: by whose stripes ye were healed. (1 Peter 2:21–24)

Then was Jesus led up of the spirit into the wilderness to be tempted of the devil. (Matthew 4:1)

For we have not an high priest which cannot be touched with the feeling of our infirmities; but was in all points tempted like as we are, yet without sin. (Hebrews 4:15)

Behold we go up to Jerusalem: and the Son of man shall be betrayed unto the chief priests and unto the scribes, and they shall condemn him to death, And shall deliver him to the Gentiles to mock, and to scourge, and to crucify him:

and the third day he shall rise again. (Matthew
20:18–19)

Then released he Barabbas unto them: and
when he had scourged Jesus, he delivered him to
be crucified. Then the soldiers of the governor
took Jesus into the common hall, and gathered
unto him the whole band of soldiers. And they
stripped him, and put on him a scarlet robe.
And when they had platted a crown of thorns,
they put it upon his head, and a reed in his right
hand: and they bowed the knee before him, and
mocked him, saying, Hail, King of the Jews! And
they spit upon him, and took the reed, and smote
him on the head. And after that they had mocked
him, and led him away to crucify him. (Matthew
27:26–31)

Then came Jesus forth, wearing the crown
of thorns, and the purple robe. And Pilate saith
unto them, Behold the man! When the chief
priests therefore and officers saw him, they cried
out, saying, Crucify him, crucify him. Pilate saith
unto them, Take ye him, and crucify him: for I
find no fault in him. The Jews answered him,
We have a law, and by our law he ought to die,
because he made himself the Son of God. (John
19:5–7)

And he that blasphemeth the name of the
Lord, he shall surely be put to death, and all the
congregation shall certainly stone him: as well
the stranger, as he that is born in the land, when
he blasphemeth the name of the Lord, shall be
put to death. (Leviticus 24:16)

Save thyself, and come down from the cross. Likewise also the chief priests mocking said among themselves with the scribes, He saved others: himself he cannot save. Let Christ the King of Israel descend now from the cross, that we may see and believe. And they that were crucified with him reviled him. And when the sixth hour was come, there was darkness over the whole land until the ninth hour. And at the ninth hour Jesus cried with a loud voice, saying, E-lo'i, E-lo'i, la'ma sa-bach-tha'ni? Which is, being interpreted, My God, my God, why hast thou forsaken me? (Mark 15:30–34)

Then said Jesus, Father, forgive them; for they know not what they do. And they parted his raiment, and cast lots. (Luke 23:34)

Then he said unto them, 0 fools, and slow of heart to believe all that the prophets have spoken: Ought not Christ to have suffered these things, and to enter into his glory? (Luke 24:25–26)

For he hath made him to be sin for us, who knew no sin; that we might be made the righteousness of God in him. (2 Corinthians 5:21)

Ye are they which have continued with me in my temptations. And I point unto you a kingdom, as my Father hath appointed unto me. (Luke 22:28–29)

The meaning of all these scriptures is that we are born into sin and Jesus who is the Son of God knew no sin. So He had to become sin for us in order that salvation of our souls could be purchased. Jesus went through all this torment and separation from His Father in order that we may never die in our sin. Not that we can do no wrong, but when we do something that we know we should not, we have an advocate that will stand in the gap between us and the Heavenly Father, whose name is Jesus. All the mistakes we make in this life is covered by the blood that Jesus shed at the cross. So when we do something against God and do not realize it before we die from this earth, all that God will see is the glory of His Son—JESUS! But if you do realize that you sinned against God, then you must ask to be forgiven, turn from that sin, and do your best not to do it again.

CHAPTER 5

Now let's get back to the Mercy Seat of God and see what the seals were all about. Jesus opened the first seal by declaring he was king and could defeat evil with a bow but needed no arrows. There was a lot of other things Jesus defeated on earth—among them were death, sickness, demons, and the last one was hell and the grave.

The second seal was the worldly government and the king that would cause death to the children aged two and under in an attempt to destroy the anointed one of God.

The third seal had to deal with religion and the way the religious leaders was handling the affairs of the temple—that they would collect from the people and what they did with the money, as well as the other performances within the temple itself, things like the sacrifices and the teaching of God's Word.

The fourth seal had to deal with the Roman Empire and the way they were treating God's chosen people.

The fifth seal dealt with the priest who obeyed God and how they were slain at the altar of God.

The sixth seal dealt with the way Jesus was treated here on earth and how He died on a cruel cross for His tormentors and gave them a chance to repent and receive salvation.

The seventh seal was opened after Jesus was resurrected. At that time, Jesus gave seven trumpets to seven angels to be blown at certain times.

In order for Jesus to accomplish this, He had to die on that horrible cross and be raised from the grave, which Jesus did on the third day. But before the seventh seal could be opened, Jesus had to show the angels of heaven that he was the one to sit on the Mercy Seat. When Jesus did this, there was silence in heaven for a space of half an hour. This is written in Revelation 8:1. And when He had opened the seventh seal, there was silence in heaven about the space of half an hour. In order to understand this, we need to look into the book of Luke in order to fill in the blanks here and to know what the Bible says on this subject.

> Jesus, when he cried again with a loud voice, yielded up the ghost. And, behold, the veil of the temple was rent in twain from the top to the bottom; and the earth did quake, and the rocks rent; And the graves were opened; and many bodies of the saints which sleep arose, And came out of the graves after his resurrection, and went into the holy city, and appeared unto many. Now when the centurion, and they that were with him, watching Jesus, saw the earthquake, and those things that were done, they feared greatly, saying, Truly this was the Son of God. This had to happen, so that the fifth seal could be identified. (Matthew 27:50–54)

> The rich man also died, and was buried: And in hell he lifted up his eyes, being in torments, and seeth Abraham afar off, and Lazarus in his bosom. And beside all this, between us and you there is a gulf fixed: So that they which pass from hence to you cannot; neither can they pass to us, that would come from thence. (Luke 16:22b–24,26)

All these verses tells us what happened to all the people that had done wrong. They were sent to a place called torment, where between them was a big gulf that no one could cross. If you went into torment, you could see the ones that was in paradise but could not call to them or cross over to even talk to them. But the ones in paradise was happy and very full of joy, for they could not see what was going on in torment.

Now on the cross that Jesus hung on, Jesus had took the sins of the world upon his shoulders, for Jesus was a man without sin. Being Jesus did this meant He had to go into torment with no way of escaping. The punishment for sin is death and separation from God. That was God's promise to Adam and Eve when Adam sinned in the garden. Adam was separated from God after he disobeyed. From that time until now, we must stay in our sin even after death, which is the second death.

Someone had to pay the penalty for man's sin. This was the reason Jesus came to the earth—to pay that penalty for man's sin. Jesus walked this earth in His earthly temple, waiting to do that which God had ordained in His soul. This is why He was arrested falsely, whipped, spat on, and crowned with thorns. All of this was the earthly punishment for our sin; then He took the spiritual punishment for you and me. This punishment was to be separated from His Heavenly Father by going into torment or hell.

But remember, Jesus was the one to sit on the Mercy Seat, for he was the Just and Righteous One who was born on earth but was also the of the spiritual realm of heaven. So how this could be, not even the angels knew. And this is what made the angels very angry. So they sent four angels to destroy the earth; but God, knowing this, had his messenger angel to stop them from doing this thing.

> And after these things I saw four angels standing on the four corners of the earth, holding the four winds of the earth, that the wind should not blow on the earth, nor on the sea, nor on any tree. And I saw another angel ascending from the east, having the seal of the living God: and he cried with a loud voice to the four angels, to whom it was given to hurt the earth and the sea, Saying, Hurt not the earth, neither the sea, nor the trees, till we have sealed the servants of our God in their foreheads. (Revelation 7:1–3)

Then something amazingly wonderful happened: Jesus is of course God in the flesh who created both angels and humans. He also created paradise and torment. When Jesus went into torment, the place that the ones who were there could not escape, Jesus gave them a chance to escape. All they had to do was believe in Him and accept the fact that He is God.

This was hard for the angels as well as those in torment, for both knew no one could escape from that horrible place. So when those who did believe that Jesus was the Son of God and God in the flesh crossed that uncrossable gulf, there was silence in heaven. With that sight, all the angels cried with a loud voice, saying, "Salvation to our God which sitteth upon the throne and unto the Lamb that sitteth on the Mercy Seat of God."

> I know that thou canst do every thing, and
> that no thought can be with holden from thee.
> (Job 42:2)

> The things which are impossible with men
> are possible with God. (Luke 18:27)

> And the Lord said unto Moses, Is the LORD's
> hand waxed short? (Numbers 11:23)

CHAPTER 6

To find out what Jesus did for this temple of mine and what he can do for your temple—by the way, temple is your body where your spirit lives. Your spirit shares the temple with another spirit, either the spirit of Lucifer or the spirit of Jesus called the Holy Spirit.

So if you wish, please, set this reading down. Get your Bible out with pen and paper. Start reading from Romans 6 and 7 and then go to 2 Corinthians 5. After that, go to Galatians 4 and 6 and also Ephesians 1, 2, and 4, as well as Colossians 3. You might as well add Hebrews 10 and 12, 1 Peter 2, and 1 John 3.

As you are reading, take notes so you can understand what I have written in these next twenty-one statements! I know this is asking a lot from you, but it will be beneficial to you. You must always go to the Bible for wisdom to understand the things that are written in those pages. Hope to see you back in this book after this assignment is finished.

Thanks for doing this.

1) I became a new creature in Christ Jesus, the Messiah!
2) I am not condemned because of my sin; Jesus forgave me!
3) Jesus died on the cross to wash away my sin!
4) I walk not after the flesh but after the spirit!
5) I am no longer a stranger or a foreigner to Christ, the Messiah!
6) I am a citizen of the household of God!
7) I am a holy temple unto the Lord Jesus, the Messiah!
8) I am no longer tossed to and fro by Satan, my enemy!
9) I am a new man created in righteousness and holiness!
10) I put off the old man and the evil deeds of Satan!

11) I put on the new man with a renewed knowledge of Christ, the Messiah!

12) I did, at times past, sowed to the flesh—sins I have done.

13) I now sow unto the Spirit of the living God—joy with peace!

14) Before I knew Christ, the Messiah, I was a child of perdition!

15) I have received the adoption to be a son of God!

16) As a son, I am an heir to the Throne of God!

17) I was in bondage by Lucifer because I sinned after the flesh!

18) I am freed by the promise of my Lord Jesus!

19) I was born into sin, and sin had dominion over me!

20) I am now born of Christ, the Messiah; sin has no dominion over me!

21) I am not under the law but under the grace of God!

In short, I am a child of the living God who has made me into a new man—a creature who is a free person. So should I sin because I am free? God forbid that I should even think that way.

You see, I am adopted by Christ Jesus, the Messiah Himself, to be heir to the throne. My hope and desire is that you believe what is written in the Good Book called the Holy Bible. My God is big enough to forgive all my sins and trespasses. Is your god that big? I sure hope so for your sake. Jesus's blood has washed me clean; I am as white as snow in my heart. What Jesus did for me, He can also do for you.

Ask Jesus to come into your heart and forgive you of your sin. He will help you to forgive others as He is forgiving you. This is the way Jesus will live in your heart and soul—with a renewed mind and spirit. What have you got to lose? Nothing but the guilt of your sin. Please do not wait until tomorrow. It may be too late for you if you do. No one is promised to have a tomorrow. When you die, you do not get the opportunity of repentance or of salvation. The Bible says: "Today is the day for salvation, for tomorrow may be too late."

PLAN OF SALVATION

What do you understand it takes for a person to go to heaven?

Consider how the Bible answers this question. It's a matter of FAITH.

F is for FORGIVENESS. We cannot have eternal life and heaven without God's forgiveness. Read Ephesians 1:7.

A is for AVAILABLE. Forgiveness is available. It is available for all but not automatic. Read John 3:16 and Matthew 7:21.

I is for IMPOSSIBLE. It is impossible for God to allow sin into heaven. Because of who He is, God is loving and just. His judgment is against sin. Because of who we are, every person is a sinner. But how can a sinful person enter heaven when God allows NO sin? Read James 2:13 and Romans 3:23.

T is for TURN. Turn means to repent. Turn from something— sin and self. Turn to Someone—trust Christ only. Read Luke 13:3 and Romans 10:9.

H is for HEAVEN. Heaven is eternal life. Here. Hereafter. Read John 10:10 and John 14:3. How can a person have God's forgiveness, heaven and eternal life, and Jesus as personal Savior and Lord? By trusting in Christ and asking Him for forgiveness. Take the step of faith described by another meaning of FAITH: Forsaking All I Trust Him.

Prayer:

Lord Jesus, I know I am a sinner and have displeased You in many ways. I believe You died for my sin and only through faith in Your death and resurrection can I be forgiven.

I want to turn from my sin and ask You to come into my life as my Savior and Lord. From this day on, I will follow You by living a life that pleases You. Thank You, Lord Jesus, for saving me. Amen.

After you have received Jesus Christ into your life, tell a Christian friend about this important decision you have made. Follow Christ in believer's baptism and church membership. Grow in your faith and enjoy new friends in Christ by becoming part of His church. There, you'll find others who will love and support you.

THE CONCLUSION

Now I can answer the first question. Do you remember what it was? How does these birds fly, and what makes them sing so beautifully? God created everything in heaven and on earth just so we can have peace with Jesus as our Lord and Savior. The birds have peace with the acceptance of nature. In this, the birds rejoice with their singing and their flying, giving praise to their Maker. Now we have that same opportunity. We ask Jesus into our heart and soul, for He is the only one who was perfect and just and who was able to sit on the Mercy Seat of God. Why is that? In this reading, as well as in the Bible, Jesus is God and sitting on the right side of the Heavenly Father on the Mercy Seat, being an advocate to the Father for us.

> In the beginning was the Word, and the Word was with God, and the Word was God. The same was in the beginning with God. All things were made by him; and without him was not anything made that was made. In him was life; and the life was the light of men. That was the true Light, which lighteth every man that cometh into the world. But as many as received him, to them gave he power to become the sons of God, even to them that believe on his name: Which were born, not of blood, nor of the will of the flesh, nor of the will of man, but of God. And the Word was made flesh, and dwelt among us, (and we beheld his glory, the glory as of the only begotten of the Father,) full of grace and truth. (John 1:1–4,9,12–14)

Just as the birds rejoice at what God did, we too can rejoice in what God has done when we accept His saving grace. Let us learn from nature—the birds, the animals, the fish, and all the plants. They all lift their heads or arms toward heaven to give thanks. With all of this, I too should not be bewildered or ashamed to worship the Creator God here on earth. If you are ashamed of Jesus here on earth, Jesus will be ashamed of you before the Father God.

Have Mercy, oh Lord. Could you please have mercy on me! I know I don't deserve mercy, but I am in sin. I need your mercy; I desire is to live in peace. This sin that I have—I know it needs to seize. I cannot promise that I will do everything right! Have mercy on me; I will do my best in your sight. What I guess I'm asking for is your salvation because my heart of sin is full of vitiation. I do not deserve your love or peace in my life. Lord, I come to you hoping I can lift you up on high! I cannot promise that I will do nothing wrong. But my hope is that you will give me a place to belong! So, Lord, would you please have mercy on me! I know you can give me life and forgive my sins. I will work for you the best way I can here on earth. But you will have to be with me, for Satan is lurking. Let me praise the name of the Lord all of my days. I will do my best to please you in all of my ways. Thank you, Lord, for this peace that is in my heart. I wish to be Your child until this world I part.

William T. Smith

Other books written by William T. Smith:

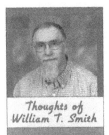

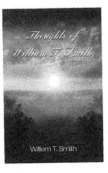

CPSIA information can be obtained
at www.ICGtesting.com
Printed in the USA
BVHW070021210821
614145BV00001B/54